Archibald's Opposites

by Phil Vischer

Tommy NELSON

Thomas Nelson, Inc.
Nashville

Art Direction:
Ron Eddy

3D Illustrator:
Aaron Hartline

Copyright © 1998
by Big Idea Productions

Illustrations Copyright © 1998
by Big Idea Productions

Published in Nashville, Tennessee, by Tommy Nelson™,
a division of Thomas Nelson, Inc.

Library of Congress Cataloging-in-Publication Data
Vischer, Phil.
    Archibald's Opposites / by Phil Vischer.
        p. cm.
    Summary: Archibald Asparagus introduces such opposites as tall
and short, light and dark, and hot and cold.
    ISBN 0-8499-1533-3
    1. English language — Synonyms and antonyms — Juvenile
literature. [1. English language — Synonyms and antonyms.] I. Title.
PE1591.V57   1997
428.1 — dc21
                           97-27880
                             CIP
                             AC

Printed in Mexico

99 00 01 02 03 BVG 9 8 7

Dear Parent

We believe that children are a
gift from God and that helping
them learn and grow is nothing less
than a divine privilege.

With that in mind, we hope these
"Veggiecational" books provide years
of rocking chair fun as they teach
your kids fundamental concepts
about the world God made.

– Phil Vischer

President
Big Idea Productions

Good morning dear class —
Archibald is my name!

Today we'll be playing
the Opposites Game!

What's that you say?
   Oh, you don't know that word —
You think it sounds silly, or weird or absurd?

I'm happy to say that I've traveled quite far
To teach you exactly what opposites are!

Here on the board I have drawn a small pea.
(Especially small, since he's not even three!)

Next on the board, and I've drawn him in yellow,
Is mighty Goliath! A very big fellow!

When things are as different
    as different can be,
We call them opposites! Now do you see?

Yes, **little** and **big**. But please, hold your cheers!
To show you some more, I'll need two volunteers!

Ah! Here they are now, and I'm thrilled to report —
The green one is **tall** and the red one is **short**!

See? More opposites!
    Isn't it grand?
But I can do more
    so that you'll understand.

This is a sunlamp to make Larry bright.
But over by Bob, it's as dark as the night!

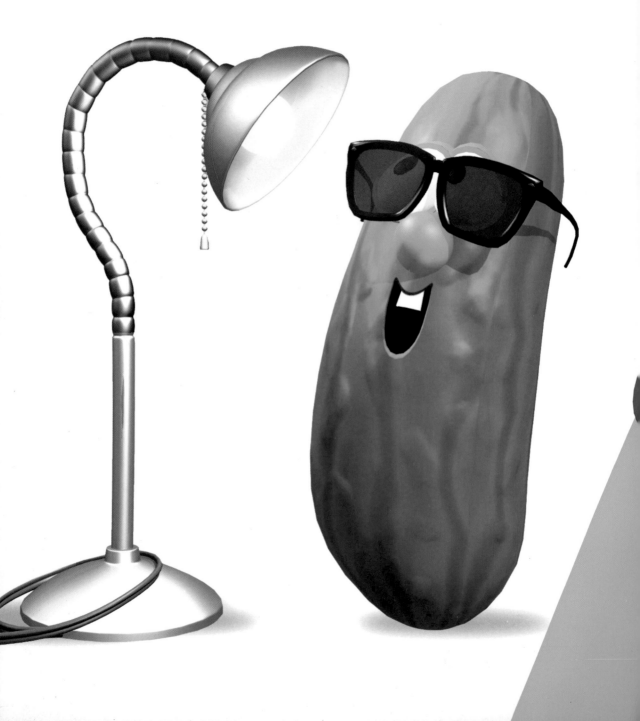

Yes, **light** and **dark**!
Oh, now isn't this fun?
Don't go away, please.
Our game isn't done!

The sunlamp will also make Larry quite **hot**.
Think of the opposite. What have you got?

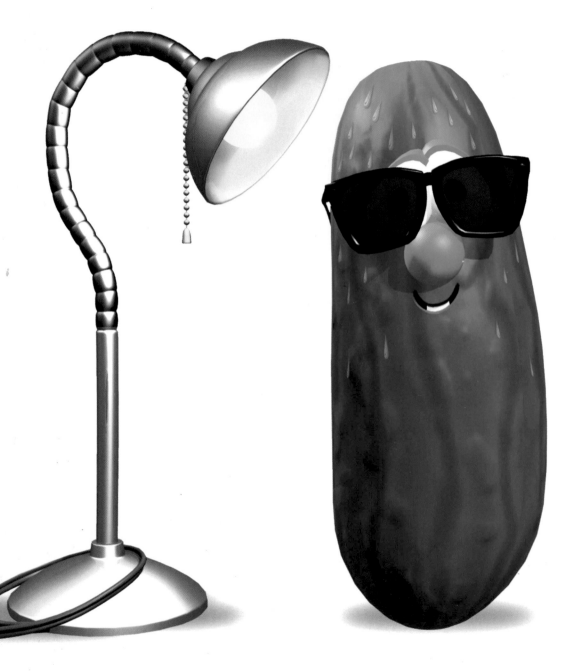

Cold is the word! Is that what you said?
Let's make Bob cold. We'll put ice on his head!

Hmm, **hot** and **cold**. Now, that makes me think
Of delicious iced tea and hot cocoa to drink!

The tea is for Larry.
  He thinks it's yummy!
Bob gets the cocoa
  to warm his red tummy!

  But wait ...

I've taken Bob's cocoa and now he feels blue!
Happy and **sad**. Those are opposites, too!

Next I'll give Larry a **sweet** chocolate pie —
While Bob gets a **sour** old lemon to try!

Hmm . . .

Someone's unhappy . . .
    and Bob is his name.
Perhaps he's not liking
    my Opposites Game?

He's coming right at me! Oh, dear — this is scary!
I think he's forgetting that pie was for Larry!!

One final lesson
before we are through —
Dirty and **clean**.
These are opposites, too.